Carmen,

Thanks so much for the support! It's a pleasure working with you & I wish you nothing but the best! Take care!

Jake

for the LOVE

short stories and poems, vol. 1

Jennifer N. SHANNON

for the LOVE

Short Stories and Poems
Vol.1

by Jennifer N.
SHANNON

for the LOVE:

short stories and poems, vol. 1

By Jennifer N. SHANNON

Copyright © 2009 by Jennifer N. Shannon.

All rights reserved. Printed in the United States of America. No part of this book may be used or reproduced without prior written consent from Jennifer N. Shannon.

For more information

please visit www.jennifernshannon.com

Cover design, title pages, and Illustrations on pgs 24, 25 and 79 by Josh Billings — www.jbillingsdesign.com

Illustrations on pgs 50 and 111 by Kwes Zackery — eKwesion media creations — www.ekwesion.com

Editing by Karen Adams — www.bookdr.net

ISBN 0-9765617-1-9

haven't said thank You in some time
not even a moment to whisper the words
life is fast
work is 24-7
no time to show appreciation

can't remember the last time I love You
was uttered
will figure in days to complain
and always find occasions to moan
the world is hard
youth and ease have passed
no time to be grateful
in the midst of sorrow

worry prevents rest
pain inverts hope
yet still standing with full mental capacity
and a portion of physical strength

You are TOO good.
Thank You.
I Love You.

~Jennifer N. Shannon

contents

introduction..........13

without you..........19

five senses..........20

daisy...............23

accident............27

scars — part 1.........48

church..............49

the closet...........52

one night............76

scars — part 2.........77

the affair...........81

poet................110

runaway.............113

dear God............136

real................139

ode to love.........140

This book is dedicated to my grandparents:
James and Ophelia Ellerbe
and Irene Shannon.

Each of you has taught me so much, just by
being in my life.
I love you!

introduction

As I began thinking about a new project, for the LOVE: vol. 1 was natural for me — meaning it just felt right. I'm far from a poet, at least I've never thought I was, but I enjoy listening to and reading poetry. When I need to evoke pure, free-spirited emotions, I use it as my outlet. In this book of short stories and poems, I wanted to explore so many topics: love, hope, God, sadness, fear, and much more. I hope you will feel the energy I intended to share. I'm sensitive about my *%ish, so don't be too hard on me! (lol)

The poems are new but the short stories have existed in various forms for some time. In the end, it was easier to write poems. Poetry may not be my "thang" but words and phrases came to me at odd times, and seemed to quench my desire to relate what I was feeling, through these broken lyrics, so to speak. Rewriting or writing the short stories was more time-consuming and difficult, because I needed to concentrate on keeping the characters aligned with the themes of the stories. Once I began I was fine, but there were times when these wonderful characters began to crowd my mind. (Keep in mind, I was also revising *Silent Teardrops* while writing *for the Love* and every character demanded and deserved my attention.)

The first story in this collection, "accident", inspired *Silent Teardrops* and was originally written way back when I was still attending USC-Columbia. It was written for Professor Ben Greer's fiction writing course. He is one the first people, other than my mom, who encouraged my writing, and that motivated me to keep putting the pen to paper.

"the closet" was written a couple years back for a fiction writing class at Kennesaw State University. For this book, the plot changed entirely, and for the better, I think.

"the affair" was also originally written a long time ago. A friend who read it way back in the day really liked it, so I felt it deserved to be revisited and revised.

"runaway" is brand-new, but I feel a very strong connection to it. It was inspired when I was driving to work one day and saw a young man walking, and the words "tattered" and "broken" entered my mind and stuck there.

I've revised these stories many times over the years, as I've learned and grown in my writing. And as a person. Over two years or five years, a person's outlook and perspective and maturity level changes and so have these stories.

I must acknowledge a few people who contributed to the production of this book: Josh, you made the cover and the illustrations speak! I appreciate your work in making my vision a reality and I look forward to working together again REAL soon. Karen, girlfriend, you really came in and put the finishing touches to what I started. You are one helluva editor. I feel such a connection to your energy. Thank you for reading my nonsense and for correcting my errors. Kwes, Kwes, Kwes! ☺ I appreciate you lending your talents and capturing them on paper for this book. (Your input and ideas greatly enhanced this book) As I tell you often, your potential is out of this world, so keep perfecting and showcasing it. Also, on a personal level, you have been so supportive and patient, watching me stare at the computer for hours on end, making me laugh when I needed a break, plus all the other little things that keep a smile on my face. Thank you! You are appreciated!

Now back to why I'm presenting this book on this day in 2009. Simply put: To let those who enjoyed *Silent Teardrops* and are eagerly awaiting something new know: I am still writing. I'm still grinding and working hard in the midst of working hard. I love it, and nothing can stop my desire or my God from working things out. I am a total believer in Him. He continually shows me, my family, and my friends, grace and mercy everyday, even in this completely insane and at times destructive world. I am so grateful. Thank You. I Love You.

To my peoples:

Keep believing, keep grinding, and stay strong! I love you Mom!!!

without you

I am afraid to let you go
Horrified to watch
your cinnamon, tan, chocolate rear
walk out the door
while I lie submerged in dreams
of happily-ever-after bliss

Fearful of the truth:
You're not in love with me
like I am with you

Terrified to feel alone again
in and out of meaningless lives
no real understanding of me

Scared to lose the taste of you
Apprehensive of missing your voice
Bothered by needing your kiss
Petrified to look for another us

Afraid to be without you

five senses

Ever watched a woman's curves?

Noticed how the darkness of her nipples seeps into almond, chocolate, pecan, vanilla or buttermilk skin-tones?

Examined the peculiarities of her
belly-button — pushed in or exposed?

Gazed at the arch in her back
and the roundness of her ass
as she lay flat on her stomach?

Touched emotions deep within
while penetrating her essence?

Felt the thrust of her waist as her body
tensed with the gentle release
of energy and fire
in the climax of the night?

Listened to her steady moans whistle
through the air while kissing her body?

Heard the sounds of pleasure and pain
along with the voice of passion
in silent, midnight moments?

Smelled love nestled deep
in the bounds of her mouth,
or sniffed the scent of the perspiration in the crevices of her breast,
or in between her legs,
or down her back?

Tasted bitter sweat before it rolls off her forehead and tips over onto the pillow?

> Licked desire off the nape of her neck
> or sucked the remnants of juices
> from her fingertips?

Ever savored the flavor of his chest or arms as your head
lay firmly on flexing biceps
between sessions of lust?

Swallowed his being or sniffed his hair during sleepy
morning hours?

Watched the length of his manhood expand
with the slightest touch?

Noticed eyelashes tighten with desire and passion during
the seams of time?

Scratched wet skin on top of a dry
layer of wanting?

Rubbed his chiseled face before kissing
smooth, thick lips?

Breathed in the hot air that surrounds an appetite for
desire and affection?

Concentrated on his pulse as
both your bodies become one
with each exertion of energy?

daisy

I love him, I love him not
He brings out the good and bad in me

Makes me laugh and cry simultaneously
Makes my inner thighs throb and
ache for his touch
but still I am unsure

I love him, I love him not
He is my best friend and my greatest enemy
I think he's crazy yet
he's the only one who understands
I'm not certain of his potential
but know it's there
He cares but at the same time doesn't

My heart beats faster when he's around
and I drag when he's away
He makes me frustrated and angry
Still I am unsure

My love, what to do?
Stay or leave, go or stay?
How to choose?
He's like air

Makes me laugh when I wish I could be mad
Makes me scream during lunchtime quickies
and evenings of passionate fights
He eats my soul with his longing for me

Touches me in a way that no other has done before
And I don't mean down there,
I mean touches a place that's

                  forever and always

      Like laying next to the one you love,
      bodies close enough to feel warmth
            yet far enough away
        to breathe in your own air

He relaxes my mind and eases my spirit
Touches me spiritually and emotionally

But still I am confused
Maybe not confused
Maybe just scared
This man has dared me to just be

Dared me,
Actually challenged me
(with my stubborn, know-it all
attitude and having-it-my-way
self) to just be with him

No questions, no doubts
Only trust and freeness

And I think I like it

I love him, I love him!

Never in a million thoughts
did I imagine life landing upside down for us.

Never in my darkest dreams could I have pictured my love
for you slipping free and falling miles away from my
heart...

for the
LOVE

accident

"Who is it?"

"Just open the goddamn door!"

The wooden door banged open abruptly but the screen door, slightly torn, remained closed as a short thin woman with pink sponge rollers stood, glaring through tiny holes.

"Betsy, now I'm only gon' tell you this one time and one time only—leave my man 'lone."

"I knew it had to be some fool at my door this time a night, but honey, he ain't here. And I don't call him. I don't want no trouble from you 'bout no man. But if you was doing what you was s'posed to be doing, he wouldn't be over here anyway."

Bernadette shifted her body weight, put her hand on her hip, and twisted her neck slightly, looking down the street like she was interested in something going on at the end of road, then suddenly reached for the handle of the broken door. It was locked. "You a scary bitch," she said with a confident grin. "Na, this yo' last warning. Yo' best bet is to leave my man alone." Bernadette, who had learned never to turn her back on an enemy, stood facing Betsy until she forcefully shut the door to the ranch style house. Bernadette slowly turned and wobbled across the small porch, then picked her way down the grey cement blocks, which served as steps.

She eased her way into the cold '79 Cadillac. She slammed the rusted-out door against the rusted-out frame, startled as always by the sound of steel-on-steel. It was almost midnight. Bernadette pulled a crumpled pack of Newport shorts from the glove compartment. The spare pack that had been reduced to five soft, worn-out sticks. She placed a cigarette between her lips and pretended to take a long hard drag. She was so nervous, just itching to strike a match. But she couldn't fire up the nicotine-filled-paper because she was 6 months pregnant with her first child. Charlie's child.

Bernadette stood 5 feet 9 inches tall, weighed about 170 pounds, and lived to love Charlie. She'd fought three other women over him. All fights she'd won. She beat Nancy Fields in the parking lot of the grocery store the day after hearing a rumor about Nancy and Charlie from one of her friends.

"Girl, guess who I saw all over Charlie the other night?" Bernadette's friend had said.

"Who?"

"Nancy. She was whispering in his ear and rubbing his chest—"

That was all it took for Bernadette to go find and confront Nancy. And it wasn't much of a fight. Bernadette grabbed Nancy while she was pushing her grocery buggy to the car. Bernadette hit her a few times, and then turned around and left as if nothing had happened.

Then there was Theresa Little, who Bernadette beat in Teresa's own yard, with three screaming children watching. One of the older kids was brave enough to call the police. Bernadette had been surprised that, as the responding officer stood between the two women, Teresa said yeah, they had a disagreement, but it was nothing to press charges over.

Ann Burns was the last person Bernadette had fought. She slapped her in the juke joint, after seeing Ann dancing with Charlie. All told, between the three women, Bernadette had blackened four eyes, given one bloody nose, knocked out two teeth, and sprained one arm.

Bernadette had beat everyone she encountered, except Charlie. He was 6 foot 3 inches and weighed about 230 pounds. Three days out of seven, he would come home after drinking and smoking in the only black juke joint in town and take his frustrations out on Bernadette. Later, on the night she beat Ann, Charlie threw a broken bottle at Bernadette, and sliced her jaw down to the white meat. He said she had embarrassed him by telling him to come home. "Don't you talk to me like that, woman, 'cause I'm a man and I do as I damn-well please." Bernadette remembered those words, as she ran her finger down the long, slightly protruding scar on her right cheek. And though she hadn't won a fight with Charlie yet, it seemed as if the more they fought, the closer she got. Last time she broke his nose.

"Stop wit all that fuss, yo' momma know what she doing," Bernadette said softly, running a hand across her stomach, trying to calm the kicking of her unborn child. She turned the ignition while firmly pressing the gas pedal. "Come on baby, crank for momma. That's it." The car responded to Bernadette's plea, and she slowly backed down the dirt driveway, then put the car in drive and crept a half-mile up the dirt road, before pulling over to the side.

* * *

Charlie was sitting on a crooked brown stool on the other side of town.

"Charlie-man. What can I pour you tonight?"

"Bubba, just hit me wit' a shot of that creek liquor you got back there behind da bar."

"Only 'cause you my best friend, but you know you don't need to be drinking that stuff. You got a family on the way."

"Just give it here. That damn woman is getting on my last nerve. I can't get none 'cause she so scared that something gon' happen to the baby. And then besides that, she don't want me to leave the house. Time I get home, she bitching if I say I'm leaving for a minute. I can't even go to the damn bathroom and take a piss without her following me."

Bubba laughed, then went to serve two other customers. It was a Wednesday night so *The Villa* wasn't crowded. The only people there were the normal drunks, who practically lived in the bar, and a few drug addicts, between fixes.

Bubba resumed his place behind the bar, near Charlie. "So man, whatcha gonna do?"

"'Bout what?"

"Not getting none? Cause I know that you ain't being faithful to Bernadette, no matter if she carrying yo' baby or not."

Charlie lifted his head from where it hung at the end of his neck, took a long hard gulp from the glass, and smiled drowsily, showing the gold cap that covered one of his front teeth.

"What's so funny?"

"Man. For the last few weeks, I been messing round wit' Betsy."

The men caught eyes, slapped hands, and gave each other a devilish grin.

"You gots to be jiving. Every brotha in this juke joint done been up in that. You must be smoking something else besides a joint. I know one thang: You best not let Bernadette find out. Cause 'member Nancy? She beat Nancy so bad, she moved wit' some of her people in New York. And man besides, Bernadette gon' be done killed you, you keep on doing her wrong. She getting tired. Shit, even I can tell that."

"Shut up, Bubba. 'Cause Bern ain't gon find out 'cause I'm gon tell Betsy that we can't mess around no more. And you know how much I want this baby. I ain't gon mess that up. Man, Bern let me feel her stomach the other night. Woo! It scared me 'cause I'm just now starting to realize this ain't no joke. That baby is real and part of me, so I ain't 'bout to mess up what me and Bern got fo' that slut. Shit, that my lil boy in there kicking like that."

Two more swigs of the brown liquor was all it took for Charlie to go off on one of his rampages. He grabbed his nappy hair and squeezed shut his eyes as if he was trying to stop tears from swallowing his face.

"Man, Bern really scare me sometimes. I mean I love her, you know but, but she like my mom. I think she gon' flip on me, 'cause right after my mom—God rest her soul—said, 'a man gon be a man,' she put my pops's own gun to his temple, after he came in the house and tried to pound on us for the umpteenth time. After that, my daddy looked smaller than a man. I mean, he wasn't my 6-foot-3 strong daddy. He looked puny and helpless. But daddy, he deserved it. Even though I done hit my ol' lady plenty times, he used to do horrible shit to us. He never showed us no love. But me, I'm different. Well at least I wanted to be. I still can be. Can't I? Well, tonight is gon' be my last time acting the fool. I'm for real. For real this time."

Bubba let his friend finish having his normal-drunken-breakdown, then came around the bar, and gently shook his shoulder. "Man, how you getting home? 'Cause you drunk as a skunk."

"I'm a-catch Jimmy. He outside." Charlie pressed both palms against his temples to ease the spinning in his head.

"You all right?"

"Yeah, I'm fine. Just need to use your car for a minute."

"Man, you messed up. You don't need to be driving nowhere."

"Come on, Bubba. I need to make a quick stop. You know how many times I done drove while I was drunk. This ain't nothing new. Shit, I done drove home while both of us was drunk and then kept yo' car overnight, 'cause you was too drunk to drive. So don't give me that."

Bubba knew his friend was up to no good but after a moment of hesitation, he tossed the keys to the '82 Buick to Charlie and then watched him stagger towards the exit.

"Be back by three."

Once Charlie made it outside, he pulled out a new pack of Marlboro's and tapped the small plastic carton against the palm of his ashy hand, tamping the tobacco tightly into the filter ends. Then he tore the plastic from around the top of the green-and-white pack, ripped off the foil, and again tapped the pack against his hand, this time farther up, near his wrist, until a cigarette slid out into his empty hand. He put the tobacco-filled paper between his lips, struck a match, then watched, slightly cross-eyed, as the fire lit the end of the cigarette.

On the way to the car, he stopped to look down into what everyone called the "pit." It was a deep drop in the land, just next door to the juke joint, where the neighborhood drug addicts went to get high. Whether it was smoking marijuana, heroin, or crack, when men and women started going down there, they soon found themselves engulfed in a pit deeper than the one in which they stood.

Charlie half-walked, half-slid down the tiny hill and then whispered into the ear of one of the men. After a brief conversation, the crippled man gave Charlie a soda bottle, a piece of foil, a pin, and a small plastic bag.

Charlie stood, inspecting the homemade crack-pipe in his hand, still puffing on his Marlboro, which hung loosely from the corner of his mouth. He examined the hole on the side of the 7-Up bottle, placed it on the ground, then took the small piece of aluminum foil and punched tiny holes in it with the pin. He picked up the bottle, placed the aluminum screen on top of it, flicked his cigarette ash on the foil, and then put the white rock on top of the ashes. Finally, Charlie tossed the nicotine stick down, mashed it into the dirt with his foot, and held the bottle in his left hand, bringing it up to about 2 inches from his lips. With his right hand, Charlie flicked his lighter until an orange flame burned brightly in the night air, then brought his arm up slowly, until the flame touched the aluminum foil. He inhaled the smoke from the hole on the side of the bottle. After a long drag he pulled the bottle away from his mouth, closed his eyes and began to shake. Charlie sunk slowly onto the ground and laid down on his side, not moving or batting an eye. About 5 minutes later, he regained consciousness, stood up, and reached into his dingy overall pocket. He tossed the crippled man two dollars before handing him back his dosage of high.

* * *

You can give a man the world and he still want more," Bernadette said aloud as she sat anxiously in the car. "My momma used to tell me that a woman is always gon' be judged by how much shit she can take from a man. But not my Charlie, he was s'posed to be different. Well he is different from my daddy, cause my daddy left us. We didn't know how we was gon' survive, but my momma got out there and did whatever she had to, to keep us going. And that's how I'll be if I have to be. But I know Charlie loves me. He just got a funny way of showing it at times. Besides," she said, looking down at her belly, "you our first baby and we gon' be happy no matter what I got to do."

Bernadette had been sitting in that same spot on the side of the road, down the street from Betsy's house, ever since she pulled out of the drive. She was patiently waiting on Charlie to go creeping towards the door, so she could stop him in his tracks, threaten him, and then take him home. Why she put up with Charlie was a mystery, even in her own mind, but she wouldn't leave, nor was she willing to put him out.

"Well Charlie, looks like you proved me wrong this time," she said aloud. "Boy, am I glad, 'cause I can't be fighting wit you when I got my little angel on the way." Once again she patted her stomach, as if giving comfort, and began the ritual of cranking the car.

* * *

"What happened, where am I?"

"Ma'am, you're in the hospital, you were in a car accident."

"What? I was just–

"Ma'am, don't worry. You'll be fine."

"My baby. What about my baby?"

"Just calm down. I have some questions I need to ask you. Are you allergic to any medications?"

"None, that I'm aware of. But—"

"Are you currently being treated for any medical conditions?"

"What?"

"Heart disease? Diabetes? Do you have high blood pressure?"

Bernadette stared at the nurse, and didn't respond.

"What about your family medical history? Did your parents have any of these conditions?"

"Yeah, but, I don't understand. What am I doing here? And what about my baby—"

The nurse raised her left hand, palm toward Bernadette, signaling Bernadette to be quiet.

"I promise, you'll get all the information you need. But again, I need to know about your medical history. Are you currently taking any medications? Prescription? Non-prescription? Legal or illegal?"

Bernadette tried to shift into a more comfortable position on the hospital bed, but that sent pain shooting up her back, so she quickly stopped moving, and stayed where she was, lying flat on her back.

"My momma had diabetes. I don't know 'bout my daddy, never really knew much about him." Bernadette whispered.

The nurse looked up from the medical chart she was writing on, her eyes momentarily full of compassion, before transforming back to normal just as quickly. "And have you had any surgical procedures?"

Sweat was secretly beginning to gather in the depths of Bernadette's palms. She tried to listen to the questions, tried to answer what she could. She gently nodded yes or no, growing more and more impatient with the list of stock medical questions the nurse-lady was reading from.

"What about my baby? Tell me bout my baby. Please. This my first and only—and I just need to know."

"Ma'am we're gonna get you admitted to a room as soon as possible. The doctor will come and talk to you shortly." The nurse began walking away.

"But—come back. I wanna know 'bout my baby."

The nurse picked up her pace as she neared the door, quickly exiting into the hallway. Bernadette closed her eyes, trying to remember what happened. She squeezed her mind back to Betsy's house, and remembered getting into the car, but couldn't remember anything after that. When she opened her eyes, the nurse was walking toward her again, syringe in hand.

"Okay, the doctor told me to give you this."

"What is it?"

"It's a sedative. It's just something to make you feel–"

"Listen, lady, don't give me no–whatever you call it. I don't want to go to sleep. I know what them thangs do. All I want is to know what happened to me and my baby."

"Ma'am, I'm gonna have to call the doctor if you don't allow me to give you this. It will only make you rest a little–"

"I'm a-tell you this one more time: Don't stick me wit' no needle."

Bernadette began to yell obscenities, prompting the short stubby nurse to quickly dart back out of the room.

Bernadette looked up at the ceiling, unable to easily move her neck from side-to-side. "What happened? I don't understand. I just turned the car on and all of a sudden, I'm here. What coulda happened?" she said to herself.

She slowly, painfully turned her head at the sound of footsteps. A balding, middle-aged white doctor walked into the room, the frightened nurse following closely behind.

"How are you feeling, ma'am?"

"I'm feeling confused. Why am I here?"

"Yes, ma'am. I'm sorry, but I have some very bad news. You were in an accident. A car accident. Unfortunately, we weren't able to save your child. There was too much blood loss."

Bernadette's mind went blank. She attempted to lift her body, to sit up, to prepare herself for the rest of the doctor's statements, but collapsed back onto the bed in pain.

"Mrs. Montgomery, please don't try to move. You were hit on the driver's side and from my understanding it was a pretty hard blow."

"Did you say my baby didn't—? Please don't tell me that. Please say something else. Say that my baby was hurt, or I lost a lot of blood, or that my baby lost a lot of blood, but don't say my baby won't make it into this world." Tears streamed down Bernadette's face.

"I'm so sorry, ma'am. There was nothing we could do."

The doctor moved toward the nurse, who was standing at the foot of the bed, and in a low voice, the two talked, one or the other pointing at a number or phrase in Bernadette's chart. The doctor paused now and then, glancing over at Bernadette. He was waiting for her to absorb the news before speaking his next words.

"The police will be coming in later to ask you some questions."

"Police? What questions? Why?" Bernadette asked through her tears and pain.

"I don't know exactly, ma'am. You'll have to wait until the police arrive. They'll be in shortly." He and the nurse turned and walked out the door.

Bernadette laid in the bed, staring at the ceiling, tears rolling down her cheeks and into her ears. She wanted to turn onto her side and wrap up into a ball, but couldn't. It hurt to move. She was beginning to feel the bruises on her arms, and noticed that her hands were shaking as she lifted them to examine the tiny grains of blood covering her fingernails and the skin of her hands. She lay there, passing in and out of consciousness.

Bernadette heard heavy footsteps and the crackling hiss of a radio. She opened her eyes and saw two policemen standing outside her door. She tried to focus on staying up, but her eyelids drooped. The effects of the accident, the unimaginable news, and sheer fatigue overtook her will to wake up. Bernadette closed her eyes, but her ears stayed open, taking in the policeman's words.

"I've never seen a case like this."

"Me, neither. So who's going to tell her?"

"I don't know." The policeman sounded just as exhausted as Bernadette felt. "How do you tell a woman who's just lost her child that the person who hit her is her husband?"

Bernadette's eyes flew open, seeing nothing but the cracks in the ceiling. She couldn't have heard that right. *Charlie?*

"What a horrible situation," the other officer said. "He's sitting in that jail cell, so high and drunk that he doesn't even know what happened."

Bernadette's heart dropped into her stomach. The voices outside continued, though Bernadette couldn't comprehend what they were saying. It was like someone had hit a mute button. She tried to rewind her mind, to go back in time, to when she had just got in the car, and was sitting alone, quietly talking to herself and her child.

"Man, I couldn't imagine, but I know it would eat me up inside if I were in his shoes." The voice of the police officer reached Bernadette again. "What are the chances that your mate will crash into you and kill your unborn child?"

"I don't know," the other said, "but there's no need in prolonging the inevitable."

Bernadette again heard heavy footsteps, now coming toward her. She felt her pulse rate increase, and the trembling in her hands spread out to the rest of her body.

The cops were so busy staring at the floor, hats in hand, as they positioned themselves at the foot of Bernadette's bed that they didn't even notice her gasping for air and the way her eyes were rolling in her head.

As the tall, slim, brown-haired cop lifted his head to deliver the bad news, the doctor and nurse suddenly charged into the room. Bernadette felt a needle pierce the flesh of her arm.

As the medicine flooded through her bloodstream, Bernadette immediately calmed and relaxed. She stopped shaking. Her head laid heavy on the pillow. She wanted to cry, but the tears wouldn't come. Then she opened her mouth, and let out a loud moan. As the sound tore through the thin hospital walls, Bernadette's tears began to flow, down her cheeks and onto her cracked lips. The people in the room appeared frozen, watching her.

Then her eyelids began to sag, and her mind began to quiet. The sobbing stopped. And as she drifted off into sleep, Bernadette unconsciously patted the place where her first child once lay.

scars — part 1

They run deep
define personalities
justify feelings
raise awareness
condemn or evoke
stagnate
motivate

> Cause hurt
> addiction
> lust
> love
> peace
> understanding
> longing
> desire
>
> Forgiveness!

church

Fingers tapping against the keys of a piano still remind me of my cousin's seasoned hands playing "Standing in the Need" one Easter Sunday morning, long ago. His voice, soft and mellow, accompanied the black and white levers, bringing tears to the eyes of those sitting in the pews.

The silhouette of a man standing tall, gray eyes, spoke deeply yet calmly to an audience of believers, the phrase "give me a home somewhere in God's great kingdom" as my granddad drew to close the morning-prayer.

The moment my pastor finished his sermon, he continued praising through song as his piercing tenor shouted "If I couldn't say a word, I'd just wave my hands." With no fear, hands from the entire congregation flew in the air. Imagine the shouts, the cries, the thoughts trailing this one declaration.

Church is more than just a building. More than the denomination associated within it. Church is about the faith and hearts of those who walk through its doors.

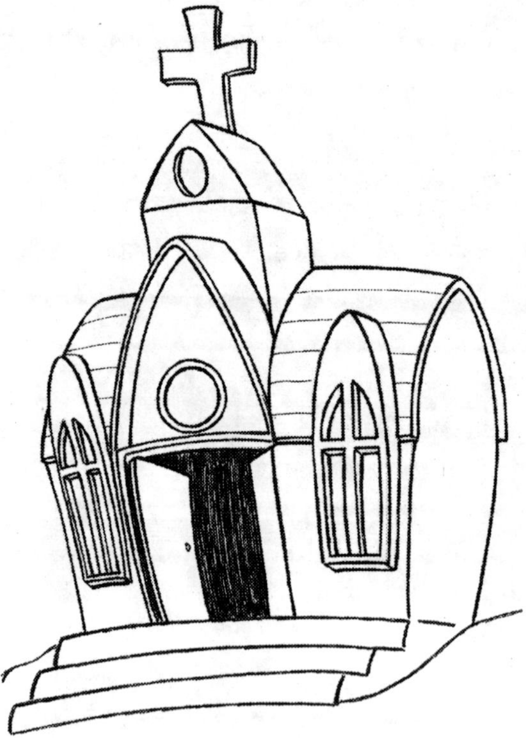

I am hidden.

Hidden even from myself.

Far from reality, far from reflection, far from truth.

I'll remain buried in this place, within reach, but too far to touch.

Until you find me.

the closet

She sat inside the 4'x6' closet, Indian-style, left hand caressing the neck of a gin bottle, right hand gripping the handle of a revolver. She gazed around the small area, taking in the two pairs of running shoes, size 8½, a black-and-gold tennis racket, and the two coats—one leather, one wool—that she'd pushed apart to create a place to sit, and that now draped her on either side. She lifted, then pressed the hole of the liquor bottle to her dry, cracked lips, practically turning it upside-down. The liquor skated down her throat, and she swallowed it with one hollow gulp, making her eyes squint and lips pucker. But she barely flinched as her chest pounded with exhilaration and exhaustion, mixed in one compact emotion.

The air inside the closet was stale as she slouched, feeling the effect of 40 percent alcohol, no chaser. Her mother's raspy voice crept into her mind and she immediately sat up straighter—as if her mother was standing in front of her—that long, demanding pointer-finger stretched toward her nose, swaying it up and down accompanied by a coarse yet sweet tone, "Sit up or you're gonna be humped over when you get old." She continued to follow the invisible instructions by straightening her spine and pushing her shoulders back. She sat as tall as possible for about two minutes, grinning with obedience, before unconsciously slumping back down into her droopy position.

Her name was Evelyn. Evelyn Mercer. A tiny woman, size 6 shoes, average tits, short afro. She wore a beautiful smile, had flawless skin, and bore a mild-mannered personality. She helped her family and friends when they needed her, but under that soft, sweet exterior, she was living a lie. And on March 5, 2001, Evelyn left her decent upbringing, her morals and values, and every other good thing she knew tucked behind her heart, in order to confront the thing that seemed to be destroying her life.

* * *

The first and only time Evelyn followed John was six months ago. She had no interest in bonding with his deceit. She didn't want the experience of becoming the obsessive wife, stalking and hiding as a means of proving what her heart already knew. One time was all she needed. She knew John had been seeing someone, but needed to witness it herself, to watch him walk into the other woman's home, before she confronted him.

Evelyn sat outside John's office in a rented black Nissan Sentra. She was disguised in a long brown wig, topped off with a fitted blue baseball cap. She waited for him to take his normal long lunch one cloudy Wednesday. He claimed he needed the extra 45 minutes. "It's the mid-way point in the week, and I need that extra push to make it to Friday," he'd said repeatedly. The statement rang in her ears while she watched John get into his car, then sit back and take a deep breath before he put the key in the ignition, shifted into gear, and left the parking lot.

John held his cell phone to his ear the entire way. Evelyn stayed three cars back for the 20 miles it took them to reach his destination in Lithonia, Georgia. The drive was easy. Fifteen minutes on the expressway, then five minutes off the exit, and John was pulling into the driveway of the other woman's home.

Evelyn stopped the car a few houses back, then turned off the engine. She pulled dark shades out of her purse and slipped them on. She slumped down into the driver's seat, the seatbelt still securely fastened across her body. The only thing that separated her disguised-self from John as he engaged in his secret life were some black mailboxes and shrubbery at the edges of a few well-manicured lawns. Evelyn remained still. She moved only after the front door of the 2-story home opened. Opened not because of a knock or a finger pressing the doorbell, but because of the sound of a car door slamming.

The woman was expecting him. Not a handyman or a colleague. She was waiting for a confidant, a lover. Evelyn eased up into a normal sitting position, straining her eyes to watch the woman who was standing in the doorway, smiling.

As John approached, the woman stepped out on the porch to greet him. Evelyn realized that John really liked her—the way he tightly shook her hand, holding it long after she let go. Evelyn watched the easy manner in which he touched the woman's back as she turned to step into the house, and the jovial smile he sported as he closely followed the woman through the front entrance.

Evelyn sat, transfixed by the scene. Craving a replay of the action. She stayed in the car, wanting to move, but unable to send the signal from her brain to make her body function. Evelyn remained in that spot, in front of a stranger's mailbox, for nearly an hour.

* * *

"Hey, John." Evelyn said, as he moved stiffly through the living room.

"Hey."

"How are you?"

"Tired."

"Dinner's ready."

"I'm not real hungry."

"John. Please. Let's just sit and try to enjoy one another's company for a change. Please?"

He stood there, eyes moving around the space, stopping briefly on a magnet stuck to the 'fridge, then to their wedding photo, hanging on a wall in the foyer. Evelyn watched him, stared at the way he searched for a way to give in without losing the silent battle they were waging with one another. She stood patiently, waiting on his answer. Evelyn knew he had already eaten. Probably with the woman she saw him greet a couple weeks earlier. Without warning, her mind reproduced the images—John's outstretched arm, the lady's smile that widened with each step he took in her direction. Evelyn closed her eyes, her feet embedded in the carpet, waiting for his response, hoping to salvage what was left of her marriage.

John glanced past this woman, his wife, who appeared to be heading out for a night on the town–tight red dress, red stilettos with black swirls, hair neatly trimmed, flawless make-up. He couldn't stop his eyes from noticing the easy and sexy side of the woman he had fallen in love with five years ago.

"Yeah. Okay. I can eat."

"Would you like a glass of wine?" Evelyn asked as they moved into the dining room, where two candles were burning on the already-set table.

"I'll take a glass."

Evelyn filled the two flutes with Riesling before scurrying to her seat.

John cleared his throat, trying to break the tension in the room. "Are you going somewhere tonight? You look nice." He forced the words out into the atmosphere, glancing down at his empty plate, then taking a sip of his wine.

"That depends."

"On?"

"On what you want to do."

"Like I said before, I'm tired. Besides, I have to be up early tomorrow. I need to get to the office to work on a presentation."

"Okay. We can stay in and do something."

John didn't say anything else, because he knew it would only end in an argument. For as long as he'd known her, she never took no for an answer. If he told her he was tired, her answer was always some version of 'get un-tired', because I want to talk or watch a movie or go out or any-and-everything else she wanted to do at that moment. He couldn't win. Her being with him was contingent on how she felt, and he resented her for that. And for changing so much. Or, maybe she hadn't changed at all. Maybe their love just wasn't enough.

In the silence, Evelyn began serving the meal. John's favorites: 10-ounce lobster tails, new potatoes, asparagus, and salad with red onions, turkey, tomatoes, and feta cheese, with balsamic vinaigrette and a sprinkling of croutons. He barely cracked a smile.

Without saying grace, they began eating. The only sounds were knives and forks scraping the plates, as they took their bites, meeting their unenthusiastic hunger.

"So, how was your day?"

"Okay. Another day, another dollar."

"Um huh."

"And yours?"

"Fine."

Silence.

"What–"

"How–"

"No. You go ahead–" John said, as they both tried to speak at the same time.

"What presentation are you working on?"

"The one for GM. I told you about it last week."

"Oh." Evelyn murmured.

And just like that, the conversation was over. Their eyes never connected again. John retreated to the bedroom, while Evelyn continued sitting alone at the dinner table. She began drifting back, in her mind, to when she'd let go of her inhibitions and lost control in another man's arms a few nights before.

* * *

They arrived at the discreet hotel room deep in Cobb County within a few minutes of one another. Without any need for words, Evelyn walked towards him, pointer finger and thumb reaching for the zipper of his loose-fitting jeans.

"Damn, Baby. No conversation tonight?"

She massaged the bulge in his pants as he leaned his 6 foot 3 frame down to kiss her lips. They quickly undressed from the waist down, never removing both hands from the other's body at once. While Evelyn's left hand maneuvered the lace panties from around her own waist, her right maintained its position on his chest. He alternated hands on her, holding her around the waist with one, pushing at his waistband with the other. Then he put both of his hands seductively along her flesh as he stepped out of his shoes and pants, one hand passionately caressing her breast while the other squeezed her butt.

They continued with their animalistic behavior until he had her pinned against the wall, her arms in the air, his decorating her waist. Once he was deep inside her, she wrapped her arms around his shoulders, and soft moans escaped into the room.

After moving to the bed, Evelyn lay underneath the man, observing his Hercules-like figure in awe.

"I love being here with you. But this is wrong. I love my husband. But—"

"But what? You don't really love him. You just don't want to be a failure in your marriage. Can we just leave this alone tonight? I don't feel like having this conversation again. If you're gonna be here with me, keep him out of it."

Evelyn's body stiffened. Her Hercules was tired of hearing excuses, and she knew that no matter what, she knew exactly what she was doing.

Once Evelyn felt him press his lips against her neck, she pushed John out of her mind and gave into her passion.

* * *

When Evelyn first walked into the woman's domicile, the air was heavy. Thick and constipated. But she shoved her mind through the space and marched further into the house. It felt different being inside the other woman's home. Six months ago, watching from a distance, was manageable, but being inside the house she witnessed her husband walk into, almost hand-in-hand with another woman was agonizing.

Evelyn slid through the plush beige carpet as she brought the gin bottle to her lips, swallowing nearly a fourth of the container while strolling through the all-brick home. She peeked into the downstairs closets, into the bathroom and kitchen, careful not to disturb the order of things. She wandered around aimlessly, never truly observing the family photos placed on tables throughout downstairs. Even as she stooped down, knees bent, balanced on the tips of her toes, gawking at a black and white picture of a smiling little girl with two braided ponytails hanging, pink ribbons tied around them in perfect bows, Evelyn saw only a blur, not the eyes of the child within the silver frame.

Evelyn continued through the well-furnished home, walking past several authentic Sass 'n Class figurines, scented candles, and a collection of books by Toni Morrison, Maya Angelou, and other great authors, grazing her fingers along the edge of the leather sectional couch, the cherry-wood end tables, and the 54-inch television. While taking a tour of downstairs, she paused, then sat down on the floor of the spacious living area, allowing the truth to register: She was in the home of her husband's lover.

She raised the bottle again, and sealed her eyes shut before dousing her throat with the powerful fluid. Evelyn contemplated long and hard on how she wanted this to go, but ironically her presence here was based on an act of spontaneity. She was lonely, frustrated, and desperate and found herself taking I-20E before she could talk herself out of it. She needed to talk to this woman. Breaking in wasn't part of the plan, but Evelyn needed to be inside when the other woman came home. She needed to frighten the woman who had caused her husband to stop having sex with his wife and nullify the relationship she tried so hard to sustain.

Evelyn planned to ask her three questions:

1. How long have you been fucking my husband?

2. Why?

3. What do you have that I don't?

The sound of those questions in her mind created tears in the corners of her eyes. Feeling sorry for herself, she started to lie down on the floor, but suddenly heard the slam of a car door and then voices growing louder, apparently approaching the front entrance. Evelyn quickly wiped her dampened face and ran to the first door she saw. It was the closet. She sat down between the coats, waiting on the woman to open the front door. But no one entered the house, and the voices faded away. False alarm. It must have been the next-door neighbors.

Evelyn sat in the enclosed space, and considered walking out the door, rushing to the car–parked a few blocks away–and getting in, going home. But she couldn't move. The liquor had settled in her stomach, was working its way into her bloodstream, taking a toll on her coordination and reflexes. She rested her back against the wall of the closet and laid the gun down, neatly, beside the glass bottle in front of her.

Outside, the sunlight had finally faded to darkness when Evelyn heard a key penetrating the lock. She quickly jumped up, snapped out of her drunken state, and slid the bottle out of her path with her left foot. She grabbed the gun off the floor.

To Evelyn's surprise, there were two sets of footsteps. Then she heard John's voice. They walked through the living area, passed right by Evelyn in the closet, and then went down the hall. Evelyn guessed they had entered the small office she had seen at the back of the home.

She could hear voices, but not the conversation. She pressed her ear against the wooden barrier, but still the sound was muffled. She softly turned the knob, lightly opening the closet door, peeking her head into the opening before tiptoeing out into the living room. As one foot tentatively touched down in front of the other, Evelyn heard cackling from the back of the house. Stopping abruptly, she found herself facing the wall over the couch. She noticed two framed university degrees, and an 11"x14" photo. The woman was shaking the hand of a man, both heads turned toward the camera, smiling, as he handed her some kind of certificate.

Once the laughter ceased and the voices were calm, Evelyn continued looking around the room, finally paying some attention to the family pictures and trophies strategically placed on stands throughout the room. She moved closer to the couch, staring intently at the certificate. She saw the words "Master of Science," then heard her name echo from the office.

Evelyn whipped around, almost falling over the coffee table as she moved quickly away from the couch, and entered the short hallway. They were talking about her. She tilted her ear confidently in their direction, listening to the voices rise and fall in an intense discussion.

"We've been through so much together." It was the woman's voice. "We have been friends since forever, so I stand by you, whatever the decision. But my professional advice is that you be honest."

Evelyn slid farther down the hallway, not wanting to miss any of the conversation.

"I'd like to tell her but I'm so upset right now." John said. "I can't stand to look at her sometimes and she doesn't even try to understand."

"Have you even attempted to explain how you feel? Remember, I asked you to write down the words which best described your feel—"

"But this isn't about her anymore. I'm over what she's done to destroy our marriage." John took a deep breath before continuing. "She's consistently made a fool of me. I'm tired of living in a home with a woman I can't trust and who doesn't respect me. I'm ready to move on. The truth is, I think I'm going to ask her for a divorce."

Evelyn's heart dropped. Divorce. She heard the two syllables of the word, playing over and over in her mind, drowning out the conversation. Suddenly, she snapped back to reality again, and resumed her pace toward the office.

She stepped into the doorway. John was sitting in a chair, hands covering his face. The woman, parked in a chair behind a desk, was shaking her head as she looked at John.

"So this is where you come while I'm waiting for you to get home."

John dropped his hands from his face, accidentally knocking papers onto the floor as his fingers brushed the edge of the desk.

"Evelyn! What are you doing here?"

"John, is this—"

"Damn right, bitch." Evelyn interrupted her. "It's me." She looked at John. "I can't believe you," she yelled, the gun hanging unnoticeably at her side.

"I can explain. It's not what you think."

"It's not what I think? You don't know what the fuck I think, but I can tell you what I know."

John stood up, positioning his body in front of the desk, awkwardly facing his wife.

"Calm down, Evelyn. Let's just talk about this. I don't know what you think you know, but whatever it is, you're wrong."

"Honestly, ma'am. It's not what you think. I'm John's–"

"I'm not talking to you, and I suggest you. Shut. The. Fuck. Up." Evelyn said calmly, looking the woman directly in her hazel eyes.

"Evelyn, like I said, it's not what you think. She's my–"

"Don't even say it." Evelyn cut in. "I can't believe your lying ass. So, this is working late for you, right? No wonder you didn't want to make love to me, you've been here fucking this bitch."

No one spoke. Evelyn was motionless, John stood twisting his head from side-to-side in pure frustration, and the woman sat, completely stunned. Finally, John spoke.

"I'm not having an affair."

"Liar."

"You're the liar. You're the one having an affair."

"What?"

"You've been cheating on me for almost a year. I know all about it, so don't even try to deny it." John said, leaning back slightly against the desk. "Not only have you been cheating, you've been lying about trying to get pregnant. I saw that research you was doing about that birth control they stick in your arm, so you don't get pregnant for five years. You don't even want children. At least, not by me." The last phrase came out in a whisper. He shifted his position again, and seemed to see clearly for the first time the gun in Evelyn's hand, the barrel pointed toward the floor.

Evelyn stood, mouth hanging open in surprise. He knew everything. Her mind began throwing up faces: John kissing this woman, who was now sitting quietly in her executive chair, and Evelyn's own tongue, flexing another man's.

"So you don't have anything to say?" John asked, his eyes moving from the gun up to Evelyn's anxious face.

"What you want me to say? This is about you. I was only getting back at you. You're the one who stopped touching me, kissing me, and now you want to put the blame on me. No!" Evelyn screamed, pulling her arm up, pointing the gun directly at John's chest.

The woman's eyes widened. John slowly lifted his arms, into the "hands-up" position, and shifted slightly forward. "Evelyn—"

The gun went off. John ducked, but the bullet had already gone over his shoulder and penetrated one of the plaques on the wall. Evelyn looked more frightened than they did, but she stood defiantly, daring them to move.

John glanced back at the woman, whose body was now deep in the chair, tightly curled into a ball, arms covering her head. He turned to face Evelyn.

"Please give me the gun. This isn't you, Evelyn. You're better than this."

Evelyn raised her other arm, and placed both hands on the pistol. She again pointed it at John's chest.

"I should have told you long ago. I've been seeing a therapist. I was ashamed. I knew that my sex drive had been changing and I, I just didn't know how to talk about it. Truth is, I haven't been able to satisfy you in some time and–"

Evelyn didn't hear anything after the word "therapist." She looked around the room, glancing at the plaque with a bullet in it, recalling the degrees and the photo on the wall in the living room.

"Did you just say 'therapist'?"

"Yes, baby." John took a small step in her direction. "This is all a misunderstanding. Dr. Turner is an upstanding therapist who wouldn't compromise her practice or our friendship for sex."

Evelyn looked at the woman, who was peeking out of her slightly opened arms. She looked hopeful, like finding solace after a level-three hurricane.

As John approached Evelyn, she dropped her arms to her sides. He pulled her close to his body and then inched back a little, caressing her face.

"I'm so sorry, John. What have I done? What have I done to us?"

"Shh. Don't say anything. We can work this out. I love you."

"I love you too."

As John embraced Evelyn tightly, she began to move the gun from her right hand to her left hand, intending to reposition it so she could match her husband's grip. But as the gun changed hands behind John's back, he shifted slightly, and it went off.

John looked at Evelyn, his face filled with hurt and confusion.

"Oh, my God. I didn't mean to."

The woman let out a piercing scream.

"Call an ambulance. Now!" John said, releasing Evelyn, and turning to rush toward the woman, now limp in her chair.

Evelyn stood, watching the scene as if it were a movie.

"Did you hear me? Call an ambulance."

John cradled the therapist in his arms, then picked her up and moved past Evelyn. He carried the woman into the living room, and laid her on the floor. He grabbed the cordless phone and dialed, making the call that Evelyn couldn't. He knelt down beside her and pressed his hand to her side, the blood seeping between the creases of each finger.

When John had finished speaking into the receiver, he eased down onto the floor and held the woman firmly as she cried in his arms. Tears plunged from his eyes while he rocked her gently back and forth, one hand putting pressure on the wound. He leaned down and kissed her forehead. "Hang in there. The ambulance is on the way. You're going to be just fine," he said softly.

Evelyn stood in the doorway, not moving, the gun now in her left hand, hanging freely at her side. John noticed it was the same black-and-brown gun he'd secretly brought into their home three years earlier. For protection. John shut his eyes firmly and bowed his head, wondering how a relationship that had started so strong had ended up like this. Destroyed in a matter of seconds, by lack of trust, lack of communication, and the very item he thought would protect his wife. Life never goes as planned, he thought, as he wiped drippings from his nose.

John opened his eyes and noticed the closet door standing open. He saw the coats pushed apart, the tennis racket, and the empty gin bottle positioned neatly beside two pairs of running sneakers.

John turned his face in the direction of the lady, relieved at the sound of sirens faintly echoing in the background. "Just hold on," he said, clutching the woman a little tighter. "They're almost here."

one night

Sitting alone at the bar.
Approaching from a distance:
tall, dark, sexy. Thick.
Eyes connect.
We meet, middle of the dance floor.
Grinding. Moving.
Slow. Fast.
Smiles, eye contact, physical attraction.
Can't blame the alcohol.
More like simple desire, freedom, lust. His body.
My place.
No inhibitions.
Great night.

                Next morning.
        Subtle smiles, shameless eyes.
    Spoken without words before he exits
            into the unknown world.
    As I walk back towards my bedroom,
         his number stares at me
            from the night stand.
          Note read (in all caps):
    CALL ME. THE NAME IS KEVIN.
   A smirk cascades onto my face.

       Time to change the sheets.

scars — part 2

I saw her standing emotionless against a brick wall. Tears inside the wells of her eyes.

Afraid of what she had become, not what had been done to her mind, body and soul.

Misguided trust and misunderstood reasons for being placed on earth, mentally sat somewhere between being born and dying inside.

From a distance, she trembled calmly as a man approached, never holding her head low, never batting an eye. She smiled, shook her head, and strolled around the corner.

Ten minutes later she returned, smile erased, looking slightly more defeated as she plopped her butt down on the pavement, legs out-stretched, crossed at her ankles.

Two more walked by and she immediately jumped up, following them with a demeanor that evoked power and grace even in the midst of bruised feet, old clothes and a diminishing spirit.

She looked familiar as she strutted away but I couldn't place that beautiful, intelligent face.

I could not tell why I knew I knew the disparity in her features.

I continued to stare but this time she left and no matter how close I followed I never saw her again.

Only an image, standing between right and wrong, up and down, fear and bravery. Torn between love and lust, being bound and freedom, confidence and no self-esteem.

She herself was a scar, one that also lives in me.

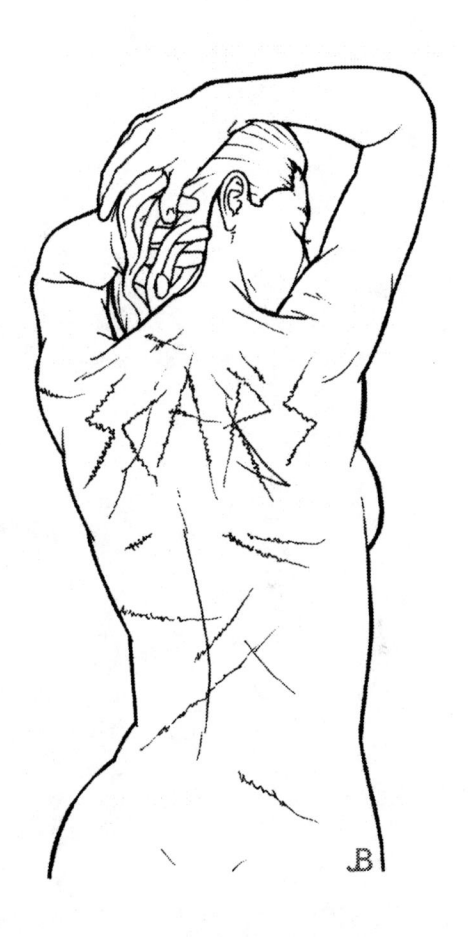

Right.

Wrong.

Truth.

Lies.

Who is to say emotions don't justify the effects?

Or cause them?

You.

Me.

Neither one willing to quiet the tongue-battle.

Neither willing to listen.

Love.

Lust.

The letters of the alphabet don't differentiate their meanings.

We do.

the affair

Tonya

"Where you been?"

"Out."

"See, I ask you a simple mutha-fuckin' question and you can't even give me a simple mutha-fuckin answer."

"Stephen, you've been drinking again, as usual, and I'm not 'bout to sit here and fuss with you. I just don't feel like going through the bullshit again. Not tonight, I'm sick of it."

"Well, whatcha gon' do 'bout it?" He paused. "Huh? Answer me. What you gon' do?"

Tonya's eyes shied away, as she tried to hide the disgust and hopelessness in her face.

"Just what I thought. Not a damn thing. 'Cause I'm the one paying the bills and making the money so what the hell can you do? Leave if you want. Go head and walk right back out that door."

"Forget it. I can't talk to you anymore and I'm tired. Tired of going through the same old–" Tonya's dismayed voice faded down the narrow hallway as she opened the linen closet and grabbed a white bed-sheet and blanket, preparing to go sleep on the downstairs couch again.

Stephen peeked his head out the bedroom door. "Thats' right, take your ass downstairs," he yelled. "I don't want you in here with me anyway."

Tonya turned around and headed back down the hall towards their bedroom. She was ready to tell Stephen where he could go and how to get there, when she heard voices coming from behind the door of her 15-year-old son's bedroom. She stopped and leaned her head toward the wooden entrance, listening. It was the radio. Tonya quickly turned back around and rushed down the stairs, leaving Stephen standing in his drunken stance, his shoulder propped against the doorway.

Gloria

"Baby, where ya been? Its almost 2 o'clock in the morning. I've been waiting on you."

"Look, I was at the pool hall with Bryan and Mike. Is that okay with you Mrs. Need-to-know-every-move-I-make? Damn."

"I figured that's who you were with, I'm sorry." Gloria said. "So, how was your day?"

"Gloria, I'm tired. And I really don't feel like talking, so if you don't mind I'm going to go get in the shower and go to bed."

Damn! Gloria thought as Leonard rushed into the bathroom and shut the white door. He didn't even notice her new short haircut and red silk lingerie set from Victoria's Secret that she'd run out and bought that very day. Gloria wanted tonight to be the night that she and Leonard made love for the first time in four months. They'd only been married three years, so the lovemaking shouldn't have gotten stale that fast. And it couldn't be because of the kids, because they didn't have any. They both decided prior to getting married not to have children. Instead, it was supposed to be Leonard and Gloria together forever, but to Gloria it seemed as if someone else had crept into Leonard's life.

Gloria plopped her head on the king-sized pillow and squeezed her eyes until the tears were forced back into the depths of her pupils. What has happened to my marriage? "All of a sudden my husband won't look at me, much less touch me," Gloria said aloud as she heard the water from the shower come to a halt. A few minutes passed before Leonard eased into bed. Once he seemed comfortable,

Gloria placed her hand gently on his back and began to massage her fingers into Leonard's shoulders.

"Stop it, Gloria. I said I was tired. Please."

"You seem tense. I'm just trying to loosen you up a little," Gloria said, inching her hands lower onto his back.

"Just stop it. I want to go to sleep," Leonard whispered, as his head sank deeper into his pillow.

Without making any objections, Gloria quickly snatched her hand away from Leonard's back, turned over so that her back was facing his, closed her eyes, and allowed salty tears to fall onto the cotton pillowcase.

Tonya

"Oh, shit!" Tonya yelled, realizing that she had just hit the passenger side of a black Lexus. She laid her head on the top of the leather steering wheel and let out another obscenity under her breath. She sat in that position, wondering how she would ever manage to save any money to leave her husband when she did things like this. Her insurance would likely skyrocket now, since the accident was clearly her fault. She barely registered the subtle soreness creeping into her muscles from the impact of the wreck, focusing instead on how many more miserable months she would have to spend in a house she so desperately wanted to leave.

Suddenly, realizing that someone else's life and well-being was at stake, Tonya lifted her head from the hard brown helm of her '87 Cutlass Sierra Oldsmobile. She watched the man in the other car as he wrapped his long slender fingers around his temples and then began to massage his head in a circular motion. Startled, Tonya pushed the heavy driverside door open and staggered out of the car.

"Are you okay?" Please Lord let this man be okay, Tonya mumbled to herself, as the man opened his door, then slowly leaned out of the car, head first, legs and feet following shortly thereafter. He seemed to take a minute to firmly plant his feet on the ground, but he didn't stand up. He just sat there, holding his face in his hands. Tonya walked over and stood directly in front of the gentleman she had just crashed into.

"Are you okay?" Tonya reached toward him, but didn't touch him.

"I'm okay. Just a little shaken up. That's all. I think," he said, with his hands still covering his eyes and forehead.

"I'm so sorry, sir. I was just...I mean, I didn't see..." Tonya said. "You came out of nowhere and I couldn't–"

"Look, I'm fine. Just a little damage done to my car. Nothing that can't be fixed." But the cloud of words didn't quite match his expression. As he tottered into an upright position, the annoyance showed on his face. His eyebrows were curled downward, wrinkles invaded his forehead, his jaw protruded as his muscles gripped one another, and his lips poked downward making a frown the most visible feature on his face. "Luckily neither one of us was going too fast," he said.

But as he fully opened his eyes and inspected the woman standing before him, his face began to soften. He was stunned at her beauty, her caramel complexion, the way her ass protruded slightly through the pair of dark slacks she wore, and the brownish micro-braids that were styled up in a clip with a few Shirley-temple curls framing her face. He refocused, taking in her facial features, then put on his best game face. "Ma'am, I'm sorry. My name is L.J. And you are?"

"Its Tonya. Tonya Williams." She smiled hesitantly. "Listen, I'd rather keep the insurance company out of this, if that's okay."

L.J. didn't respond, but simply got up and walked around the rear end of his car, to the side that Tonya had hit, as Tonya followed closely behind. He stooped down to the ground, examining something on the exterior more closely. He looked over at Tonya's car. It had little damage on the front end, while L.J.'s passenger door was severely pushed into the passenger seat.

"There's a lot of damage done to my car," he said. "How do I know you can pay if we don't go through the insurance company? This is going to cost a couple thousand to fix."

Tonya nodded her head, in accordance with his rationale. He didn't know her, and she probably couldn't pay for the damage to his car unless it was in monthly installments.

"L.J. is it?"

"Yes, ma'am."

"You're absolutely right. Let's handle this the right way. I have insurance and I'd rather your car get fixed properly. That's what you pay car insurance for, right?"

They shared an awkward chuckle, followed by a moment of complete silence. Apparently, one of the spectators who saw the accident had called the police, because the silence was quickly broken by the sounds of sirens in the distance.

"Well, looks like someone already called the police," Tonya said. "Do you need to go to the hospital? You should probably go, even if you're not feeling any pain. As a precautionary measure."

"I think I'll do that."

Again they both stood, alternating intense eye contact with staring at the ground, or checking their watches, as if to determine whether going to work was still a feasible option. Once L.J. was strapped to a gurney and loaded into the ambulance, and the police had written Tonya a ticket, she drove to work.

By the time she got home that evening, Tonya remembered it was Friday. When Stephen came home they would eat dinner, her son would ask to go to the football game or over to a friend's house, and Stephen would pretend to be the best husband in the world just so they could have sex. Tonya hated Fridays. She could handle the bitching and fussing every other day of the week, but having to let Stephen touch her and kiss her was almost repulsive. Pretending to enjoy sex with a man she hardly liked was as tiring as a fat woman running up a hill.

And she knew that being tired wasn't a valid enough excuse for this week. It had been three weeks since the last time they did it. The first week, she said her period was on and the next week her son was grounded and had to stay home. But there would be no such luck this week. As soon as Stephen walked into the bedroom after work, he apologized for the night before, sat down beside her, and began rubbing her back.

"Let me give you a massage. That accident is going to have you sore."

Tonya's muscles tightened as his hands begin to rub her neck. Five minutes of contact was all she allowed, then she excused herself to the bathroom. When she came out, Stephen was unbuttoning his shirt.

"Tonya, I'm sorry about last night. You know how I get when I drink. I don't mean half the shit I say."

Tonya walked to her closet, not even acknowledging his second attempt at an apology. "Look," she said, "I need to go downstairs and cook something. I thought you were going over Jason's tonight to help him fix something."

"That's tomorrow. Besides, I can run and get us some Chinese food so you don't have to cook."

Tonya didn't object. Stephen picked up dinner, and they had a half-way normal conversation while watching a movie. The night went better than she expected. Her son had gotten home from the game and Stephen had dozed off waiting on Tonya to come to bed. As Tonya fluffed her pillow and happily laid on her side, Stephen turned over and moved closer to his wife.

"Tonya, I love you," he whispered, his lips scratching her shoulder blades, while his fingers chafed her thigh. Tonya didn't say anything, just succumbed to her husband's advances. She laid flat on her back and tried to focus on something other than what was going on in her bedroom. Stephen became more aggressive as he kissed and fingered his wife. Without an excess of foreplay, he climbed on top of Tonya and tried to penetrate her. Tonya attempted to loosen up; her arms flung along side her knees and her legs gapped open as wide as possible. She took a deep breath as Stephen shoved his way inside her. He huffed and puffed for about 5 minutes, then a final grunting thrust signified that he was done. Tonya completely relaxed her muscles while Stephen fell over into a deep coma-like sleep. Another ten minutes passed before Tonya eased her numb body out of bed and went straight to the shower.

She sluggishly placed her feet on the silky porcelain until she was standing upright, allowing the hot steamy water to course over her body. Then she began to lather her arms and legs with the sweet and soft smell of her favorite body wash. Tonya scrubbed until her entire body hurt; until her skin was pink and raw and her hands and feet were wrinkled like the face of an 80-year-old woman. Finally she sat down, then slid down deep into the tub and thought about what her life had become. It was depressing. She had the same routine: Go to work, come home, cook, clean, be mom, wife, child to her husband (at least that's what he thought), and supposably love every minute of it. She was tired. Tired of the same thing. She had been living this life for the past 20 years. But now, her son was close to becoming an adult, and for the first time since she could remember she felt like living. Her family meant the world to her. And even though it seemed that she was consumed by habit and what everyone else needed and wanted, it felt safe. This was the way it had been her entire adult life and that seemed normal. Not right, but normal.

Tonya stepped out of the shower, letting her body air-dry. She put on a green satin house robe and watched it suction around the fullness of her hips, butt, thighs, and breasts. She decided to head downstairs to finish the glass of wine she'd left sitting on the end table earlier. As her foot touched the first step, the phone rang. She rushed to grab the cordless before the ringing awoke Stephen.

"Hello." Tonya failed to keep the annoyance out of her voice.

"Hi. Is this a bad time?"

"No, no! Is that you Gloria?

"But, of course. You remember me? I'm the beautiful black woman you ran into a few weeks ago."

Tonya laughed. Nearly two months earlier, she'd almost slaughtered some woman with her shopping cart in the seasoning aisle at the grocery store.

"I'm so sorry," Tonya said, walking around to make sure the woman was okay.

"It's okay. My cart caught the worse end of the stick," Gloria said, wearing a frown while she inspected the woman who was rapidly approaching.

They both stood silently for a few seconds.

"Again, I'm sorry. I wasn't looking, just pushing and completely let go."

"It's okay. I wasn't paying any attention either."

Tonya stepped back to her buggy and rotated it in the opposite direction, while continuing to scan the shelves.

"What were you looking for? Maybe I can help you find it," Gloria said, not wanting to be the kind of bitch who held a grudge for an in-store buggy accident.

Tonya turned back around to face Gloria, her face still tense, but relieved.

"Bread crumbs. I'm making chicken parmesan, and I was looking for bread crumbs."

"Really? My husband has been asking me to make that, but I never have. Is it easy to make?" Gloria said, feeling compelled for some reason to keep the conversation breathing.

"Yes. Oh, I see them now, they're back in the other direction," Tonya said, forcing a smile. "My name is Tonya, by the way."

"I'm Gloria."

"Well, Gloria. I'd be happy to share my recipe. It's not a big secret or anything, just something I got out of a recipe book."

As other people maneuvered around the two women, snapping glares and whispers, Tonya and Gloria exchanged phone numbers. It was a strange way to begin a friendship, but they'd spoken three times already since the buggy accident. They were still nicking the surface, though, with small talk and chit-chat.

"I'm sorry for calling so late," Gloria said, "but I just need someone to talk to."

"Hey, anytime. What's up? You're not trying to kill people in the grocery store these days, are you?" Tonya heard a friendly laugh and a sigh of relief from the other end.

"Not today, but if you ask that question next week, my response might be a li'l different."

"Why?"

"Oh, nothing. I just need to get out. I haven't done anything in a while and I need an outlet. You know what I mean?"

"Hell yeah. I don't get out much either. With my son and husband needing my undivided attention all the time, I normally stay around the house." Tonya settled herself comfortably on the couch, wrapping a chenille blanket around her legs.

"I don't even have a child but I understand what you mean," Gloria said, allowing a sarcastic chuckle to emphasize her point.

"I can't remember the last time I had time for me."

"We should get together," Gloria blurted out.

"Sounds fine to me. We can do dinner almost any weekend. Does that work for you?"

"Yeah, that's fine."

"Good. Well…"

"Tonya," Gloria interrupted, "Can I tell you something?"

"Sure."

"I think my husband is having an affair."

Tonya didn't know what to say. Her eyes were drawn to the picture on the muted televison screen illuminating the living room. The character in the TV western had just pulled his gun on some bad guy. "Oh," she said, taking a sip from her glass of red wine.

"I just don't know what to do. I can't confront him. Its just not me, to do that, but I also know we can't stay in this marriage, not communicating with one another. Not doing anything with each other. He doesn't seem to want me anymore." Gloria waited on Tonya to comment, but she didn't. She continued to sit, staring at the flickering screen, wondering at how opposite their lives were. Tonya had just had unwanted sex with an oblivious husband. If only he didn't find her attractive any more! Would their problems be compounded or lessened? Either way, it would mean they both wanted the same thing. Out of the marriage.

"Are you still there?"

"Yes, I'm here. I was just thinking. I mean, my husband and I have had some problems. I don't know what I would do if I thought he were cheating. At this point, I can't even say. It's a tough situation to be in, Gloria, and ultimately you have to do what your heart tells you."

On the other end of the phone, Gloria leaned her head forward, pulling the receiver away from her face, tears welling. She wanted to share these things with someone else, her own faults that she hid deep inside, away from outsiders. And as Gloria listened to Tonya speaking, she realized that they were in a similar place. Tonya had just admitted without admitting that she and her husband were the same: Stuck between where to go and why, unable to take the necessary steps to preserve or destroy what once felt like finding a diamond buried in a hay stack.

The conversation brought a sort of relief to the women. Besides both of them being in difficult marriages, they bonded in a way neither of them had done in some time. How refreshing it was to be honest with someone else about their fears instead of holding them inside, waiting on those trepidations to inadvertently seep out into the atmosphere.

It was almost 1:30 am by the time they hung up. Tonya slowly crawled into the queen-sized bed with a half-smile. Half because she was miserable in her own bed, her own house, but on the other hand, happy and relieved there was someone else who could identify with her grief. Happy that they could shed heartfelt tears together like they had tonight and not be ashamed. Relieved that another human being was feeling as hopeless and as desperate she was. But mostly glad that God had found a way to bring these two individuals together, apparently in order to make each other's lives a little more bearable.

Leonard

It was 2:45 am and Leonard was just creeping into the bedroom. He slipped out of his favorite outfit: Gap denim jeans, a gray cotton V-neck T-shirt, black Timberland boots, and a gray starter cap with Chinese letters in the center. Leonard stood over the right side, his side, of the bed and began to nod as he glanced over at his wife's curvaceous body. She looked so soft and beautiful, yet he couldn't bring himself to place his large longing hands on her. It had been so long since he'd felt himself inside of her. He stood there, allowing his mind to wander back to when it was a ritual for them to please each other in the morning before going to work, at night before going to bed, and anywhere in-between. But not since that day.

December 3, 1998. That was the day he decided to surprise Gloria in Charleston, South Carolina, where she'd gone on a business trip. When he stopped at the red light on Main Street and pressed the button to change to the soothing sounds of Rachel Ferrell on his newly installed 6-disc CD changer, he saw Gloria and another lady run into a gray building. He parked, ducked into Smith's Florist, and came out with six long-stem red roses. He crossed the street and approached the building with a smile that quickly diminished as he took in the protesters standing off to the side, holding baby dolls and posters, chanting, and praying aloud.

His eyes shifted back and forth from the building entrance to the little group, trying to keep out the awareness that this gray mass of concrete was an abortion clinic. He dropped the roses to the ground, ran back to his car, and waited. Three hours passed before his wife slowly exited the building, arms crossed tightly over her stomach. He watched motionless in disbelief until his wife and the woman disappeared around the side of the building.

He got out of the car and headed into the building. The waiting room chairs were filled with women and men of every race and culture. Leonard approached the window, but kept glancing around the room at the faces of people who sat comforting one another, or chatting, or flipping through the pages of a magazine as if they were in an airport lounge, waiting for their flight to be called.

"Can I help you sir?" The thin woman said. "Sir, can I help you?"

"I just thought that, uh, my wife was supposed to have a, an–". The woman looked suspiciously at him. He started over. "My wife has a one-something appointment, I think, but I can't remember and –"

"I'm really not supposed to give out that information sir. Sorry."

It didn't matter. Leonard didn't need to have someone confirm what he saw and felt in his heart. He had seen her enter and exit, had seen the tears that streamed down her face, and the woman who had escorted his humped-over wife to a car around the corner, parked strategically in the opposite direction of the protesters a few hours earlier.

Leonard was in complete shock. He couldn't believe Gloria could destroy a life, part of him, without one thought as to how he would feel. Yes, they had decided not to have children, but deep down Leonard was feeling incomplete without a child. He wanted to pass down his genes and personality and care. He had even mentioned it to Gloria a few times, had asked her jokingly if she really wanted to grow old and have no one take care of them. They'd shared a laugh over that, but the idea never materialized into serious discussion. Why didn't she trust him enough to talk with him? To ask him to not only support her in the decision, but to rely on him to be her rock? Why would she lean on someone else?

It had been a little over a year since Leonard had witnessed Gloria's teary yet deceitful eyes, and now all he wanted to do was find the right time to tell his wife he was ready to separate. He wanted to tell her that it was not that he didn't love her, but he needed to clear his mind. He wanted to find a way not only to forgive her, but to forgive himself for not intervening when he had the opportunity.

Leonard forced his mind to snap back to reality, to the present, and after watching the covers slowly move up and down from his wife's silent gasps of air, he got into bed, left leg first, until he had scooted his body underneath the thin top layer of sheet and was laying flat on his back. He knew Gloria was awake but he didn't want to start an argument so he stayed in that uncomfortable position, the same way he stayed in his marriage.

Tonya

Kissing L.J. was different. She didn't feel like she was cheating while her mouth was intertwined with his. Tonya was in the honeymoon phase, stuck smack-dab in the middle of "if it's wrong, I don't want to do right." Completely smitten by his charm and overwhelmed by his smile. She was intrigued by the innocence and mystery he carried. She'd caught him more than once drifting to some far-off mental place, but she didn't ask for more information than he offered to share. He only contributed brief glimpses into his past and hopes for the future. He never mentioned a wife or girlfriend, but Tonya knew he had someone. Someone who had cut him with a knife, stuffed her hand inside the wound, and refused to let him heal. Tonya felt for him, and wondered if his life was as complicated as hers.

When Tonya got in bed that Friday midnight, after lying for the past two days about being at a teacher's conference in North Carolina, she felt herself anxiously rub her inner thighs as she thought about the time she spent wrapped in L.J.'s arms. He knew exactly when to be aggressive and when to be gentle. He waited on her, wasn't fast or impatient. Let his lips caress everything in his sight, plus a few things that weren't. She had never been touched that way. Had never kept her eyes open to watch a man. Never had a man flick the light switch to the "on" position and tell her how beautiful she was and that all he wanted to do was look at her. Tonya continued touching her body until Stephen realized she was there, and threw his arm around her waist.

"Hey, babe. You're home," he said. "How was the conference?" He asked, attempting to shake the grogginess from his voice.

"It was okay," Tonya said, quickly turning her body in the opposite direction.

"We're glad you're home. You know, that son of ours can eat. I had to go to the grocery store and I ended up spending like 150 bucks on junk he wanted: cereal, chips, soda. And he's already eaten almost everything I bought," Stephen said, grinning into the dark with a mixture of pride and marvel at how much food their son had actually eaten over the past two days.

"Why do you think I'm always in the grocery store? That boy eats everything he can find plus some."

"I really missed you. It's lonely in this bed when you're not here. Its cold and I like having your soft body to rub up against," Stephen said, moving closer to Tonya.

She laid uncomfortably still, knowing exactly where this was going.

"I know we haven't been on the best of terms lately, but I'm ready to try. I realize how much I need you and can't lose you," Stephen said, leaning up on one arm, looking down at Tonya's profile, his other hand resting on her side.

She didn't say anything. Just lay, waiting on this moment to pass.

"I've been a real asshole lately, so I understand if you don't want to talk to me right now. But these couple of days apart have let me know exactly how much I value this family and our life together. So, I've been thinking that we should go on a little trip in a few weeks. Wherever you want to go, just the two of us. You pick the place."

Tonya sighed. "I'm tired and need to get some sleep. Its been a long week, so let's just talk about this tomorrow. Okay?"

"Okay," Stephen said, lying his head back on the pillow, then sliding his body firmly over to his side of the bed. "Yes, we can talk tomorrow," he reiterated, resting uneasily on his back, hands folded behind his head. He found it impossible to go to sleep, knowing he was in danger of losing his wife.

Gloria, Tonya, Leonard

Gloria was quietly waiting in the living room. She heard a car door slam and peeked out the window to see Leonard glowing brighter than a 100-watt bulb. She hurried to the front door to meet him with an equally vivid smile.

"Hi sweetie!"

"Gloria," Leonard said, startled, as if she shouldn't be there when he opened the door. "We need to talk when I finish upstairs," he said, strolling pass Gloria, not even looking into her face.

What just happened? Gloria thought as she watched the back of Leonard bolt upstairs and disappear into the bedroom. He looked so happy walking up the steps, but as soon as he saw me, his whole facial expression changed. She sat on the couch, anxiously waiting for him. Leonard stayed in the bedroom for about 15 minutes, then he ran down the stairs with a piece of luggage in each hand.

"Leonard. What is going on? Where are you going? Why do you have those suitcases?"

"Let's not make this any harder than it has to be, Gloria. I am leaving. I can't stay with you anymore. I've been feeling this way for a long–" He stopped himself, then glared at her. "How could you?"

"What do you mean you're leaving? Gloria couldn't stop the tears. She knew this argument had been coming for a while but never in a million years did she think it would be today. "And how could I do what?" Just as she was about to beg him not to go, the doorbell rang."

"Look, Leonard. Please. Let's just talk about this later. I told you my friend Tonya is coming over today. Please put your things down, at least until after she leaves," Gloria said, wiping away tears and rushing to the door at the same time. Leonard put down the suitcases and retreated toward the back of the house.

Gloria opened the door and greeted Tonya with a crooked smile that let her know immediately that something was wrong. Tonya questioned Gloria silently, with an equally awkward facial expression, then followed Gloria down the hallway toward the kitchen. As Gloria motioned for Tonya to take a seat at the kitchen table, Leonard stepped into the kitchen from another doorway.

"Ah, Leonard. This is my friend, Tonya." Gloria said, sniffling as she turned towards him, to make the introduction.

Tonya took in L.J.'s chiseled features, trying to control her own. She struggled to appear normal but her eyebrows instinctively curled inward and water began clouding the area in the corners of her eyes.

"Tonya, this is my husband, Leonard."

Leonard stood quiet and rigid, unable to hide the surprise on his face.

Gloria twisted her head back and forth between them, recognizing their connection through tell-all eyes.

Leonard finally looked away from the women, strode down the hallway, grabbed his bags, and marched out the front door.

poet

I am not a poet.
My sentences don't rhyme nor do I read my work with hard inflections of pitch in humming song-like motions.
The beat of the drum, purr of the sax, pluck of the guitar, don't play soft melodies behind my voice
 nor does it compliment my routine.

I am not a poet.
My words don't always lie
underneath prolific or
enthusiastic meanings.
The letters which form my expressions
don't follow an orderly path.
They curve and twist, specializing in
nothing and everything.
My phrases don't sway to a beat
nor do they always carry
a political or hidden message
deep within its lyrics.

I am not a poet.
I prefer not stand in front of a crowd
using hand gestures and sassy dialogue
to allude to pages of a personal notebook.

The microphone doesn't interest me,
nor do the snaps of fingers mid-air
after a great performance
give me an unforgettable high.

I am not a poet.
I am a person who loves
poetry, music and words.
The way they can be transformed into
synonyms, verbs, nouns, or prepositions
with one swipe of the pen.
How they can sing a sad song,
speak life in the midst of doubt
and soothe minds through
truth or fiction.

I am not a poet
in the traditional sense
but I am poet...
I use words to intensely
give meaning to blank pages.

I am not only a poet,
I am most importantly a writer...

I left you behind to find me.

Walked away from all I knew to be better.

Searched and Found.

Found love. Found me.

But now I'm back and ready to live again.

runaway

The door stretched quietly open as his size 10½'s lightly touched down on the front porch. He quickly jumped off the brick platform and then started moving faster towards the edge of the yard. He paused when he reached the point where he would cross over onto the road. He looked back at the house, feeling a pair of eyes calmly watching through closed blinds, before turning his face forward, in the direction of darkness and uncertainty.

He ran on thick gravel for what seemed like hours. Eyes red and body soaked. His t-shirt had a rip in the middle and was spotted with dots of blood. His jeans were wet, the knees black. His lungs released heavy air as he ran up the hill and followed the deep curve of the road. He had been in constant motion for nearly 15 minutes, and after tripping over a branch lying in the road, he slowed down to a fast-paced walk. His mind was running faster than he had been, but all he could think about was getting out of that house. This wasn't the first time he thought about running, but it was the first time he had actually done it.

When he reached the end of the road he tiptoed into the woods, occasionally firing up his lighter, to guide him along an overgrown path to what he considered his safe haven. This place of shelter was an old abandoned shed deep in the woods, about a mile off the main road. He had found the place by accident, the first time. He had been walking home from the bus stop one day and instead of turning towards his house, he'd hiked down the road, and then kept going, right past the "Road Ends" sign. He'd strolled through the leaves, listening to limbs break under his feet, to the squirrels hop between trees, and to the strange sounds coming from deep in the woods. After about 30 minutes of aimless wandering, he'd seen the building and rushed to see inside it. No fear had entered his mind as he'd pushed open the wooden door and crept inside. Once he'd sauntered in, he felt this abandoned place was all his own. Like it was put there for him to find and keep all to himself.

Tonight was different. This wasn't just his hideout anymore, a place to hang out when things got bad, this had now become a place to lay his head until he could figure out what came next. He looked down at the torn t-shirt and then pulled it over his head. He tossed it on the floor beside him and examined his arms and chest for bruises and cuts, noticing the old scars. He'd finally done it.

Finally stood up to the man he had feared all his life: His dad.

He had gotten tired of the fights, tired of watching his mom block punches with forearms thrown up in front of her face, or a knee lifted up to deter a hit to the stomach. So this time he stepped in. He stood in front of his dad's 6'5 frame like a man and dared him to beat his mother again.

"Boy, you better get out my face before I fuck your li'l ass up," he said aloud, mimicking his dad, standing in the exact same position, facing down the thought of his dad being in his presence.

"Don't hit my momma no more."

"I said, move before I hurt you."

"Not until you leave her alone."

He felt his mom's hand touch his tightened fist, "Baby just do what he say. This between me and yo' daddy."

"You best listen to her."

"If you such a man, hit me, you coward. Stop beating on a woman and hit me."

In the blink of an eye, his dad had raised his fist and swung for his face. He ducked, and caught his dad's lip with a right-hand hook, and then punched him again with his left until he fell to the floor. He dropped down on top of his father, pounding whatever was in his reach until anger had transformed to hate. That hatred made its way to his wrist, fingers, hands, as he wrapped them around his dad's neck and began to choke what life he had left out of his body. His mom sat in the corner crying, begging him to stop before he killed him. He focused on his dad's eyes as they rolled into the back of his head, but couldn't let go.

* * *

"Earth to Jay. Baye, wake up," Karen said, snapping her thumb and forefinger together in front of Jay's dreamy eyes.

"Yeah, yeah. I'm up. My mind was just somewhere else."

"What were you thinking about?"

"Nothing, really. I don't know."

"Well it had to be something. And nothing good. You're jaws were clinched, eyes tight. You looked like wanted to kill someone."

"Okay. So what? Why are you worried about it? It's over now," Jay said as he shifted his body up into a sitting position on the bed.

"I'm asking about it because this isn't the first time we've been having a conversation or watching TV and your mind traveled to some scary place that you aren't willing to talk about." Karen paused and leaned out of the bathroom door a little bit, trying to look into Jay's face, although he avoided her eyes by staring aimlessly towards their wedding photograph hanging on the wall near the armoire. "You scare me sometimes and I'm worried about you."

"Don't. I'm fine," Jay said, slipping his legs from underneath the bed-sheets and creeping to the bathroom door to peek in on his wife. Karen twisted the hot and cold chrome facets until water flowed into the sink. She bent her head down and cupped a handful of lukewarm water and threw it into her face. She lifted her head, eyes closed, wet eyelashes holding buds of water, and reached into mid-air, where Jay met her hands with a towel.

"Baby I'm fine," he said easing his body directly behind hers. "I just have some things on my mind. I haven't been home in a long time and now I have to go because my dad is on his deathbed. A man I haven't spoken to since—I mean, I don't even know how I feel about it. All I know is that I have to go. Hell, I haven't even seen my mom or family in 'bout 10 years so this is scary for me."

Karen didn't speak, simply looked at Jay's reflection in the mirror before leaning back a little and watching them both, as a whole. She knew it was more than that but didn't push. The one thing she hadn't liked about Jay when they first got serious was his disconnection with his family. Only occasional phone calls to his mom, plus the $100 he sent bi-weekly, which he'd tried to keep a secret, were the only teasers he offered up about his past.

"Okay," Karen finally said, grabbing the toothbrush and toothpaste, looking away from the faces glaring back at her.

Instead of loosening the grip he had around Karen's waist, Jay pressed his pelvis against her butt and leaned down, tenderly nibbling her neck.

"Jay. We've got to get on the road. What are you doing?"

"Shhh," he said, lifting the Victoria's Secret t-shirt above her panty line while rubbing his hands from her rear to her stomach. His fingers slipped into Karen's panties, feeling her wetness before quickly removing his hand, moving his fingers up to be drenched by his mouth. Karen's moans were soft as she reached back to touch the increasing length of Jay's manhood. She quickly stepped out of her panties, widened her stance, and waited until she felt Jay enter her from behind. Their bodies rocked back and forth, their fingertips grinding into the mirror, condensation blooming beneath them.

Karen opened her eyes, watching as her features tightened with each thrust. She examined the way Jay's faced was filled with hurt and pleasure. One of his large hands pulled her size C breasts together before reaching back down between her legs. She squeezed her eyes closed, feeling a throbbing that indicated she was reaching that point of ecstasy. Jay could feel her body talking to him. His movements became faster, his pants deeper.

"Oh shit," he screamed as his body jerked in one final motion.

As their bodies calmed and the heat surrounding them subsided, Jay laid himself on Karen's back, feeling his heartbeat and her breathing flow into one succinct motion.

* * *

When they pulled into the driveway of the all-brick home, Jay didn't flinch. He sat dazed by nothing but the structure before him, almost startled by how familiar things felt. The memories swarmed within him even though years had passed. He gripped the steering wheel just as hard as he had tugged at his own father's life on that night. His hands quickly became drenched in perspiration, while his heart nearly beat out of his chest. He shut his eyes and tried to determine the best way to get out the car. Karen didn't move either. She was caught up in her own emotions, afraid to find out why Jay was so secretive about his family; why he left home and hadn't returned until now. She turned her head in his direction, noticing how stiffly he sat, barely blinking, barely breathing. He was frozen. As scared as she. Perhaps even a little more afraid of what was on the other side of the door to the home in front of them.

She finally shifted forward, wanting to face whatever came next. She gently touched Jay's shoulder, just enough to wake him, just enough to let him know she was there.

"You all right?"

"Yeah." Jay said. "Might as well go in, right?"

Karen nodded, slowly pulling the lever to open the door. Jay sat still for a few more seconds before following suit and slowly forcing his body out into the warm South Carolina air. Even before the horn sounded from the click of the doors-lock button, the door from the house flew open.

"Lawd, there go my baby. Jay, if you don't get up here and give yo' momma a hug," the woman said, gleaming with joy. Jay was equally excited, rushing towards her, arms outstretched.

"Momma. It's so good to see you," Jay said, picking up the 5'7" woman, his large arms forming a dark brown belt around her flowered housedress.

"Boy, you best not never wait this long to come home again."

Jay put her down and then just stood there with a simple smile, almost as if he were a teenager being spoiled rotten by his mother.

"Baby, you look so good. You really been taking care of yourself."

"I been trying. You look good too. How you been?"

"Baby, momma all right. I'm just happy to see you. Can't believe it's been nine, going-on-ten years since I seen yo' face," she said, softly touching his jaw, then grazing her fingers along Jay's chin. She was amazed at how her son had grown. He was a man now. Had always been one, in a way, but now he wasn't the teenager who ran away from his problems. Now he was a man who had come back to face them.

Caught up in the moment, both Jay and his mother had forgotten about Karen. She shyly remained near the car, waiting on the right time for her to extend a greasy hand to this woman she's heard almost nothing about.

"Ahh, mom, this is my wife, Karen."

"Wife? Baby! Why you didn't call us? We woulda come," his mother said, walking firmly toward Karen, recognizing her discomfort but paying it no mind, and embracing her with weakening arms. Karen hugged her back, relaxing within her hold.

"Baby, my name is Janie, but you can call me Ma."

"Yes ma'am. It's nice to meet you."

"Same here. You a pretty thang, wit' all that hair. Now y'all come on in this house. I done cooked and we been waiting," Janie said, leading Karen by the hand toward the house, then grabbing Jay's hand on the way.

As Jay was being tugged forward, he stopped, bringing both the women to a jolting halt.

"Baby, you all right?" Karen asked, looking back at her husband.

"Yeah. I'm cool, just need a minute."

Karen watched Jay's eyes begin to water. Janie released Karen's hand and made her way back to her son.

"I know it's hard but this is still your home. Besides, yo' daddy took his medicine a little while ago, so he won't be up for hours," Janie whispered as she leaned in towards Jay's face.

Jay's eyes were glossy. Even looking at his mother, seeing her soft features and graying hair encourage him, he still didn't move. His feet felt like they were stuck in the ground, underneath a few layers of dirt, with grass sprouting up around his ankles. He tried to lift his legs but couldn't shake free. Then, he found himself moving his heavy, stiff feet, but he was turning in the opposite direction, then he was running down the street.

"Jay," Karen called after him, but he didn't slow or turn back. She called his name again, her voice drifting around Jay's head, but it didn't seem to enter into his eardrums, or if it did, it didn't connect to his brain.

"Baby, he gone."

"Gone where? Is he okay?"

"He be all right. Just need to clear his head, I reckon."

"I don't understand," Karen said, dropping her arms by her side, feeling helpless.

"I guess he never told you why he left and stayed away."

Karen shook her head no, gazing in the direction Jay went. "How could he just leave like that?"

"Well, baby I wish I could tell you exactly what happened but I can't."

Karen opened her mouth to speak, but Jay's mother placed her pointer finger in front of Karen's mouth before any words could be released.

"The reason I can't give you the details is: They ain't mine to give. Jay only wanted to protect his family and something terrible happened in the process. It was unfortunate, but it wasn't his fault. My son has always been a good boy, just had to grow up faster than some, and was forced to become a man while his own daddy was in his life but acting the fool. Janie grabbed Karen's hand, and rubbed the top of her dark skin in a soothing motion before speaking again. "Jay just need a few minutes to think through how he gon' step back into a house he ain't seen in years and how he gon' look at a father he damn-near hates."

Karen nodded, resigned.

"Now, come on and let's go in this house. I'll fix you a plate."

* * *

By the time Jay reached the abandoned shed, he was winded and sweaty. He placed his arm against the corner of the building and rested his head on his forearm. With his eyes closed, he felt like he was positioned back in front of his house. The thought sent shivers up his spine. He shook the reflection out of his mind and stood up straight, to face this old place he sometimes called home during his adolescence.

With a little effort, Jay was able to push open the door and he saw right away that no one had touched the place in his absence. No one had fixed up any part of it, nor had anyone tore down any part of it. The edifice was steadily falling apart due to natural causes, the wear and tear of the elements eroding it bit by bit. Jay entered anyway, searching for a little bit of quiet for his mind.

Jay's movements were calculated as he entered the space, stepping slowly onto patches of dry brown grass and weeds, maneuvering around the old tractor that had been there when he first crossed the threshold in 1995. It was even more rusted now, with small flakes of color scattered around the sides. He continued, careful not to go in too deep too quick, but sneaking along as if he might disturb someone sleeping in the corner of the shed, far away from life.

He looked down and noticed a can lying on its side near a tarnished, dirty spoon and a piece of cloth. The items seemed familiar, and he knelt down to look. Yes, they were his. His can of pork-n-beans, recognizable for what it was only by a tiny piece of the label that fell off when he lifted the can off the ground. He glanced over at the soiled shirt, thinking back to the moment he had ripped it from his body, throwing it to the ground in anger. He peered at the piece of fabric, filthy with dirt and blood. He stared at the shirt, and without warning, started to cry. For the first time since that night he shed tears. Jay's mind raced back and forth from the past to present.

"All I wanted as for him to stop. Stop beating up on her. To stop making us watch, stop making us afraid," Jay mumbled through tears, as if he were that 17-year-old kid, defending his actions. "Why did I have to go back? Why? I hate myself for it." After the words tore from his mouth, he made his way out of the dusty shed. When he stepped out into the woods, his arms began flailing around his head, fighting off a swarm of gnats gathered outside the door.

He ran heavily, nearly falling, as he followed the path his footsteps had created, back home. When he opened the door, memories stormed his mind.

"Where is he? Where's my dad?"

Karen and Janie rushed into the living room from the kitchen, hearing what sounded like a teenager's voice echoing from the front of the house.

"What's wrong baby?" Karen asked, realizing that it was Jay, but his voice had transformed back to that of a child's.

"I just need to know where he is."

"I'm in here, son." A faint voice made its way out of the guest bedroom.

Jay took a deep breath and marched in to see his father, a man he hadn't laid eyes on in nearly 10 years. He hesitated only for a moment in the doorway, then made his way closer to the bed. When he stared into the old man's face, he could see that death had indeed fallen upon him. Each strand of hair on his head was gray, wrinkles were poured on his face, and his body appeared frail and small. He looked far older than his age.

"Son, you finally came back home."

"I came back cause I needed to. I needed to see you before you died," Jay said, his voice fading when it arrived at the last word.

"Janie, come light me a cigarette."

With the same obedience as always, Janie, who had been standing in the doorway observing, walked over to the dresser and grabbed the box of Camel Lights, plucking one from the pack. She eased past Jay, and placed the cigarette in his father's mouth. Scrapping a match on the corner of the night stand, she put the flame to the end of the stick.

"This place is still the same." Jay said. "Even half-dead, you still got complete control over my mother. I never understood that. Never understood how a man could treat a woman so bad and that woman still break her back to make him happy."

"Baby, it's not like that."

"Janie, you don't have to explain nothing to him. 'Specially not about our relationship."

"Some things never change."

"How you know? You been here for all of two minutes and you think you know something," the old man said, coughing out his smoke.

"I can tell 'cause Momma still jump when you call. Still moves at the speed of light when your mouth opens."

"That's what she supposed to do. I'm laying here dying, ain't I? So why wouldn't she get me a cigarette if I ask? I'd do it for her."

"No, you wouldn't. You never loved my mother, nor did you love us."

"I did love you, just had a messed up way of showing it. But I'm sorry. I really am. I don't want to fight with you but I imagine that's the only way we gon' move on," he said, pushing himself up toward the headboard, his arms shaking has he elevated his butt. Then he dropped slowly back down onto the mattress. "I haven't been the best father. But right now, I'm saying I'm sorry. I'm not just saying that 'cause of this situation, but I truly am sorry for everything that happened. After that night, I had to–" He couldn't finish. Tears creaked from his eyes, sliding down his face, before his long fingers sprinted to his cheeks to prevent them from dripping onto his neck.

"After that night, you had to do what? Say it daddy, say it!" Jay screamed.

"Jay, please don't do this. Please," Janie moved toward her son, taking his arm.

"No Momma, let him finish. Why did you have to bury your youngest son, daddy? Why?"

"Because of you."

Karen stood just outside the door to the room, her arms folded across her chest, listening to the past unfold.

"Yeah, I'm the reason he was shot but I didn't kill him. Did I Momma?" Jay asked, looking intently into his mother's face, seeking confirmation for his words.

"No. It wasn't your fault, baby. It wasn't yours at all. John was gone long before he was shot. He was a sensitive boy. Always taking stuff to heart. He was in this house with us too long. Too long for his own good and we didn't even realize it. Parents know they children, but sometimes we don't do what's best for them. Sometimes we so caught up in our own lives that we don't realize we hurting them. So no, it wasn't your fault, it was ours."

Jay physically felt like he was back in that moment. He took a step back from his mother. "See that night, when I came back, I was so tired, I just wanted to get in bed." He looked at his father. "But what did I see but John pointing a gun at you? And me being stupid, I tried to save you. Save you!" Jay took another couple of steps backwards. "A motherfucker who beat my mom in front of us damn-near our entire lives. And when I tried to take the gun from him—" Jay stepped backward again, and found his back against the wall. He slid down slowly, his hands covering his face. "And the sad part is, I still don't know why I did it. Guess I didn't want him to go to jail for killing the man that I should of killed when I had the chance." Jay removed his hands from his face and looked strangely at his father, as if he was seeing him for the first time. "John didn't deserve to die that night, but you did. You deserved to die over and over again." Jay gave a short laugh. "I guess my prayer has finally been answered."

Nobody moved. The old man seemed to have forgotten that he was smoking. His arm hung limply off the side of the bed, the cigarette now burned down to the filter, the cigarette ashes long since fallen onto the floor. The silence was loud. The truth was breathing in all the oxygen in the room, suffocating everyone in it. Jay wiped his nose and then slowly raised his body until he was standing on two feet.

"I can't do this anymore. I been carrying the weight of this secret on my soul since I walked out that door ten years ago. And I just can't do it no more. I'm tired. I grew up too fast. Became a man in a house where 'the' man acted like a boy. I promised myself, I wouldn't turn out like you and that's the one thing I'm going to hold on to. Not being like you, but being better than you."

"Son, you've always been better than me."

"I don't need you to tell me what I know. I came here to get my peace and I got it. Now I can go on and live my life." Jay said. "Thanks daddy, 'cause without you, I wouldn't have known who not to become."

Jay turned and walked out the door, to find his wife standing in the hallway. "Come on Karen, time to go."

Janie ran after her son, lightly touching his arm. "Baby, please tell me you're not leaving already?"

"Momma, I'm leaving. But not for good. I'll be back, but I need some time. I need to get out of this house. I've finally said what I needed to say. So I can move on now."

"Just remember that we love you. I love you, Jay, and so does your daddy. No matter what, he still loves you."

Jay embraced Janie, closed his eyes and felt John's presence light the room. "I love you too, Momma."

Janie gently stroked Jay's head, before letting him go and wiping evidence of her own tears away from her face. Karen hugged Janie, unable to force any words to leave her mouth.

"Baby, you make sure he come back, now," Janie said quietly, directly into Karen's ear.

Grabbing Janie tighter, Karen simply nodded her head. She let go and trailed Jay to the car. From the guest room, as Janie waved at her son and his wife from the porch, Jay's father whispered, "I love you too, son."

* * *

Two weeks later, Jay returned and buried his father next to John.

dear God

It's me again. Asking for all the things my mind can imagine, thanking you for all the things You've given so freely. Contemplating the length of time it's taken me to write this. I apologize, realizing I have taken for granted my life, health, strength, family to call in time of need. My job in this time of financial insecurity. Clarity of thoughts: Yes I still have sense enough to thank You. And call You even after long absences.

In the midst of this prayer, my mind travels to places I can see only when I close my eyes. Refocus. This is time for me and God to reconnect. I tell Him about my life, where I've gone wrong, things I wish I'd done differently; quick to add that I have no regrets, as if He doesn't already have this personal insight into my life. I continue with, I have a confession or two. I'm scared of death. Scared not only of my own passing into the unknown but those who are important to me. I am afraid not to have those I'm closest to be there when I need to hear their voices. Who will I have in my life to keep me sane if those I know and love are not here?

Another fear I have is being alone. At times that's exactly how I feel. Like I'm in this world and no one hears me. Friends seem to be fewer and fewer as time progresses and even those who are my friends aren't always there when I need them. Next subject!

There are several truths I've learned — Keep living, keep laughing, tomorrow is not promised, life "ain't" fair, You did not give me the spirit of fear (though I still worry more than I should) and You are in control even when life seems to be in complete turmoil.

Now I'm drawing a blank. Not on all the wonderful things You've done. No, I can jot down an entire notebook of things You have done for me even when I don't deserve one line of Your goodness. No, I'm drawing a blank on where to go from here. WHERE DO I GO FROM HERE? I'm here but not sure where I belong. Standing before You, waiting on direction. Unable to move until I hear from You. Not sure where I'm going, if others will embrace my words and accept my thoughts. Frightened of being a failure and equally afraid of being a success. All I ask is for You to help me find my way. Help me see what's next. Help You shine through me. Let my actions speak louder than words.

As always, please continue to protect me, my family and friends from dangers seen and unseen. I am nothing without You. I need You more than I ever did and imagine that I'll continue to need You more as I grow and experience the sadness and happiness this life will offer. And believe me I look forward to the good times. (I thank You in advance)

I guess this is it for now. We'll talk later. Thank You. I love You.

real

Genuineness is few and far between, during these times of idealistic thoughts about how it should be.

Reality is distorted, real love is almost extinct.

Like is confused with lust and everything else is a means of being comfortable. What happened to passion? Honesty? All flushed by the wayside in an attempt to look happy.

We have become too holy to live, too scared to believe, and too self-confident to pray. When did we learn to stop loving and needing each other? Standing in the midst of fake smiles and pretend conversations, everyone attempting to be unique in a world of followers.

To be one's self is almost unheard of but there are still a few. Yes, there is still some realness inside this vast place. Still those who see the moon, grass, sky, and appreciate the beauty of colors...

To be continued...

ode to love

It's as discreet as the wind whisking cool air on a hot day.
Gentle.
Subtle.
Yet you know it's there.

It's fulfilling.
Nourishing.
Everlasting.

As profound and extensive as the sky;
No reach can touch it.
No end in sight.

Can't feel without it.
Can't breathe without it.
Can't live without it.

Love.